Heartbeats

Do you know
'I, I, me oh my'?

        I,   I,   me oh my!

Sing the song.
At the same time, tap the hearts and feel the pulse.

    1   2   3   4

1. Ask a partner to tap the hearts as you sing the whole song. *(I, I, me oh my!)*

2. Tap the hearts (the pulse) and sing the song with your 'thinking' voice. *(I, I, me oh my!)*

Feeling the pulse p.34

'ta' and 'ti-ti'

Here is the pulse:

And here is the rhythm of 'I, I, me oh my':

ta   ta   ti - ti   ta   ti - ti   ti - ti   ti - ti   ta

1 While your partner taps a steady pulse: Speak this rhythm.

ta ta ti-ti ta
ti-ti ti-ti ti-ti ta

2 Then tap the rhythm.

3 Then play the rhythm on a percussion instrument.

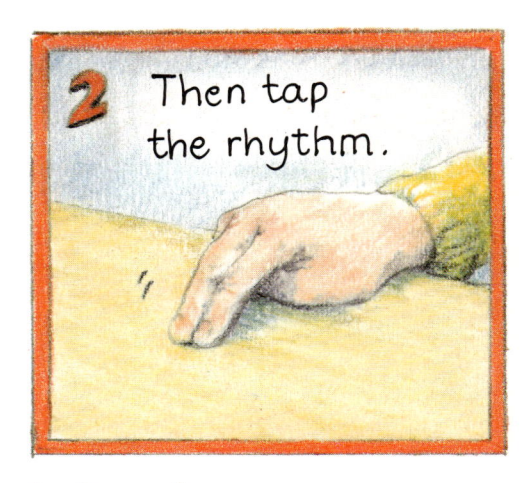

Using only 'ta' and 'ti-ti', make up a new rhythm of your own.

Can you speak it?

Can you tap it?

Can you play it on a percussion instrument?

2   Reading   p.34

Strong beats

John the blacksmith is working hard as he sings his song.

His hammer rises and falls in time with the pulse.

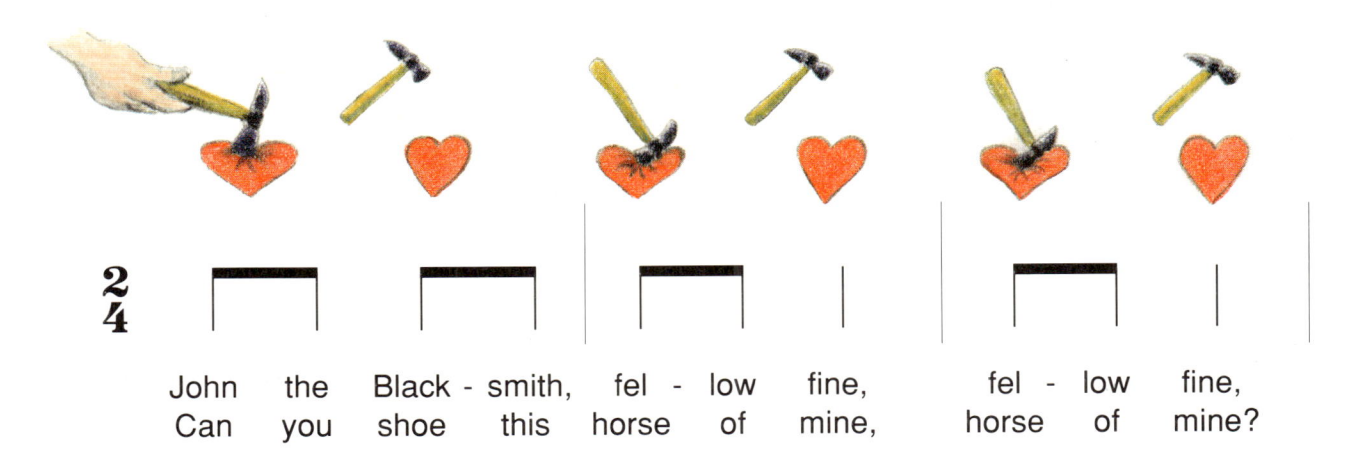

$\frac{2}{4}$

John the Black-smith, fel - low fine, fel - low fine,
Can you shoe this horse of mine, horse of mine?

Sing, or speak, the song.
Can you hammer like John, as you sing?
Now speak the rhythm names as you hammer:

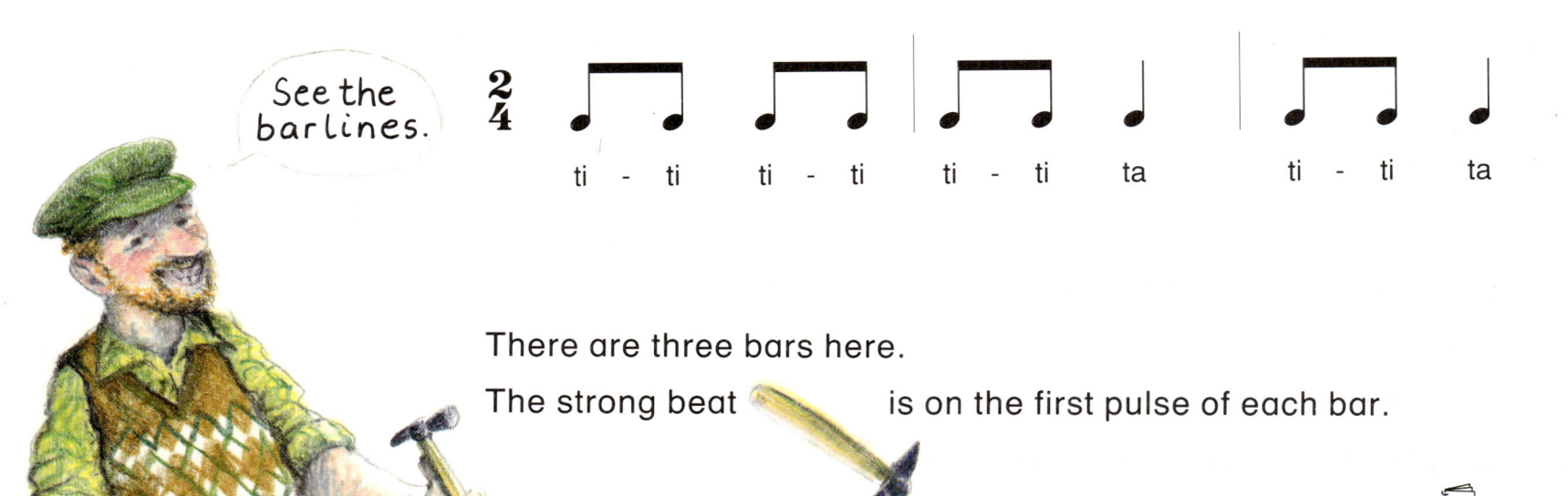

See the barlines.

$\frac{2}{4}$

ti - ti   ti - ti   ti - ti   ta   ti - ti   ta

There are three bars here.

The strong beat is on the first pulse of each bar.

Feeling the strong beat   p.45

soh, me and lah

'I, I, me oh my' uses two singing names – 'soh' and 'me':

s m s s m s s m m s s m

Speak the rhythm only.   **Tap** the rhythm only.   **Sing the melody**, using the singing names.

The next melody uses *three* singing names – 'soh', 'me', and 'lah':

s m s m s s l l s m

With your partner:
Speak the rhythm only.   **Tap** the rhythm only.   **Sing the melody**, using the singing names.

soh   soh
  me   me

Introducing rhythm-solfa   p.47

Listen to the band

The band is playing in the park today!

Can you sing the melodies the band is playing?

Tap a steady pulse as you sing.

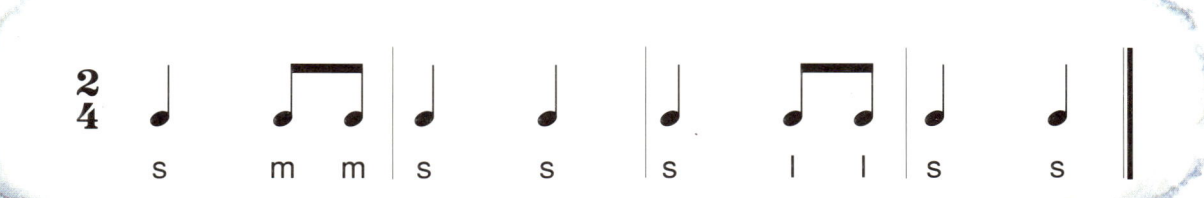

$\frac{2}{4}$ s | m m s | s | s l | s s ‖

$\frac{2}{4}$ m m s s | m m s | l l s s | m m m ‖

$\frac{2}{4}$ s | m | l l s s | s | m | l l l ‖

$\frac{2}{4}$ m l s | m m s | m l s l | l ‖

Reading rhythm-solfa   p.48

Take a rest

Tap a steady pulse and speak the rhythm names:
Take a breath, or blow gently, for each rest.

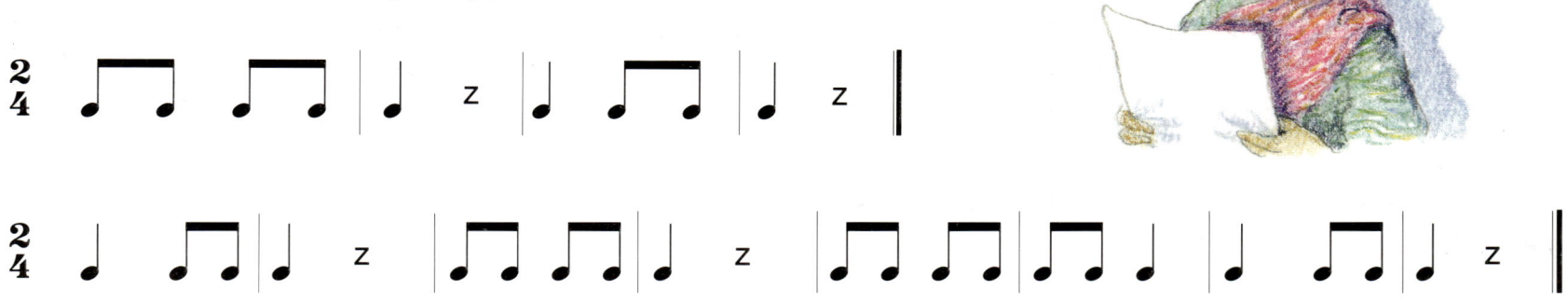

Choose a percussion instrument, and play both rhythms.

Play each rhythm twice – the first time in a slow tempo, the second time in a faster tempo.

1 Now make up your own rhythm, using ♩ and ♫ and z

2 Speak it, tap it, and play it on an instrument.

3 Now write it down.

4 Ask a partner to speak, tap and play your new rhythm.

Rhythm reading with z   p.49

Tunes with rests

Sing these melodies, taking a breath (one pulse) for each rest:

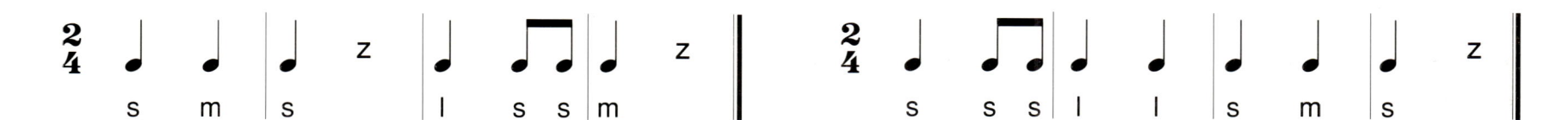

Here is a new rhythm:

Speak the rhythm. Tap the rhythm.

Choose singing names (lah - soh - me) to sing with the rhythm.

lah
soh
me

Write your melody down.

First copy the rhythm,

then write the solfa letters underneath.

Rhythm-solfa with z   p.51   7

Composing your own melody

Now you are ready to compose your own melodies.

1 Make up a rhythm to fill four bars (2 beats to each bar). Include a rest, if you like.

$\frac{2}{4}$ | | | | |

2 Speak your rhythm and write it down.

3 Speak.... and then tap the rhythm you have written.

ta ti-ti ta ...

4 To a steady tempo, choose singing names (lah-soh-me) to sing with your rhythm.

5 Write your singing names (l-s-m) under the rhythm. Now you can see your melody written in rhythm-solfa.

$\frac{2}{4}$ ♩ ♫ | ♩ 𝄽 | ♩ |
   s m m   s

Ask a partner to read and sing your melody.

Can you write more melodies in this way?

8 Composing l–s–m melodies   p.51   7

Phrases

Sing this longer melody. It has eight bars.

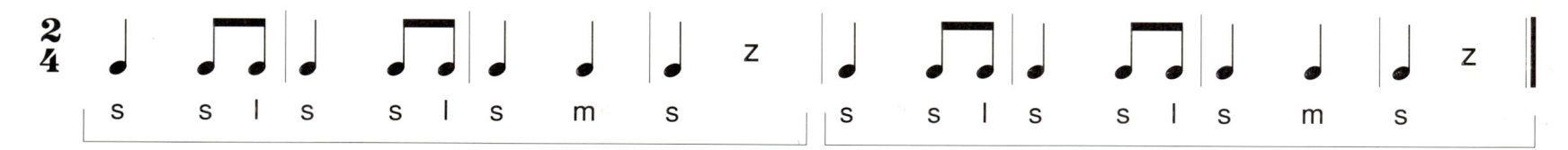

[Musical notation in 2/4 time with solfège: s s l s s l s m s | s s l s s l s m s]

The melody has two phrases.
Each phrase is four bars long.

Sing phrase 1, then sing phrase 2.
Are they the same or different?

Here is another 8-bar melody:

[Musical notation in 2/4 time with solfège: s s s s s m s l s m | m l s s s s l l s m]

This melody also has two phrases.
Each phrase is four bars long.
Sing both phrases.

Are they the same or different?

Now compose a lah-soh-me melody
with two 4–bar phrases which are **the same**.
Then compose two phrases which are **different**.

Reading and composing longer melodies   p.51   7

The 5-line staff

These melodies use three singing names – 'soh', 'me' and 'lah'.

Speak the rhythm.
Tap the rhythm.
Sing the melody for a partner, using singing names.

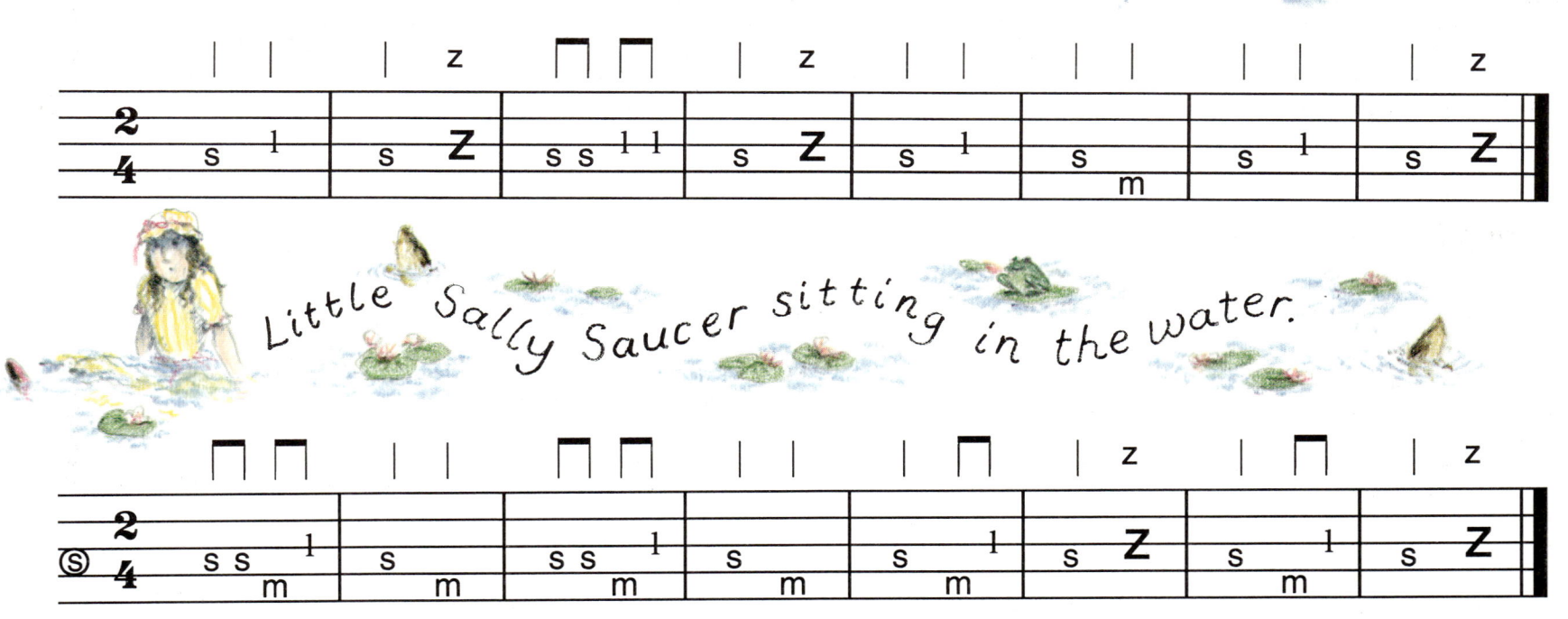

Can you see the ⓢ at the beginning of the line?

It tells you where 'soh' is on the staff.

A song for a long journey

On this page, ⓢ is in a new position on the staff.

These swallows are getting ready to fly south.

Can you make up some words to their melody?
– a song for their long journey.

In the next melody the rhythms join the notes on the staff.

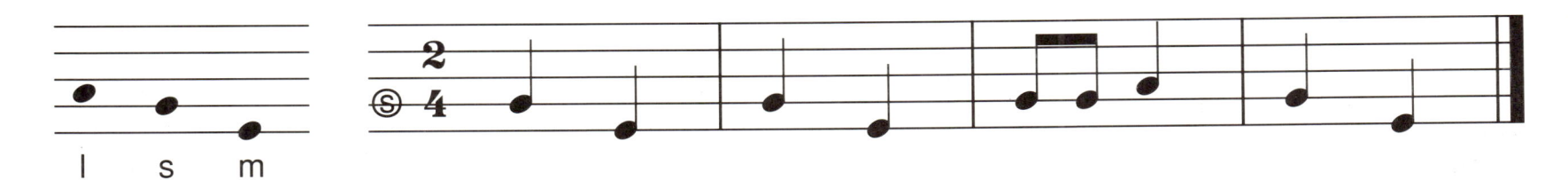

Tap a steady pulse and sing the melody, using the singing names.

With a partner, decide on a note for 'soh'. Sing the melody together.

Now choose a different note for soh. Again sing the melody together.

Staff notation p.57

Sharing games

You will need the help of a partner.

Check the position of ⓢ before singing.

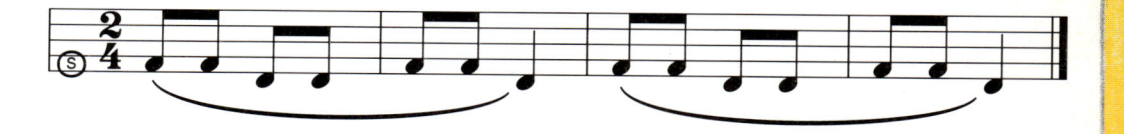

Can you see the curved lines? They are phrase marks.

1 Sing the melody using singing names (solfa). You sing the first phrase; your partner sings the second phrase.

2 Tap a steady pulse. You sing the 'soh' notes in the phrase; your partner sings the 'me' notes.

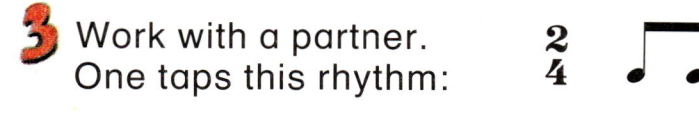

3 Work with a partner. One taps this rhythm:

At the same time the other sings this melody (using solfa names):

4 Tap a steady pulse.

You sing the quarter notes (♩) in the melody;

your partner sings the eighth notes (♫).

Preparing for two-part work   p.57

From solfa to staff

Here is a rhythm:

Speak the rhythm.
Tap the rhythm.
Write down the rhythm.

1. Choose solfa names (lah-soh-me) for the rhythm.

Lah? Soh? me?

Try to put a me-lah jump in your melody.

2. Write your solfa letters (l-s-m) under the rhythm.

Now your melody is written in rhythm-solfa.

3. Using Writing Sheet 8, prepare a new staff, like this:

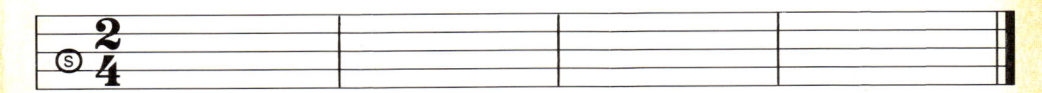

Look carefully at the position of Ⓢ

Then write your melody on the staff.

Now you can see your melody written in staff notation.

Converting to staff notation p.58 7 and 8

Lucky dip

Choose one of these melodies. Sing it to a partner, using solfa. Ask your partner to point to the melody you sang.

With your partner copy out these melodies and also the melodies you both wrote for page 13.

Cut out each melody so that you have five pieces of paper.

Place the papers in a box and play 'Lucky Dip'.

Sing the melody you find.

John the Blacksmith

Here is our song about John the Blacksmith:

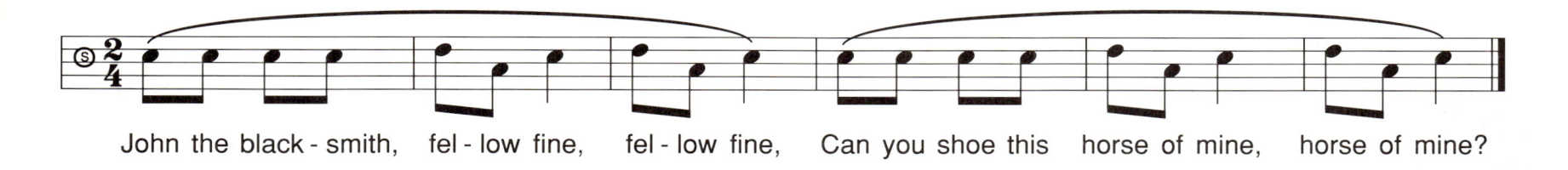

John the black-smith, fel-low fine, fel-low fine, Can you shoe this horse of mine, horse of mine?

Tap the rhythm.
Sing the melody to solfa.

The melody has two phrases.
How many bars are there in each phrase?
Are the two phrases the same, or different?

Sing the song to the words.
How fast is John's hammer working?
Try the song at different speeds.

What do you think is the best tempo for John's hammer?
What does your partner think?

There are lah–me jumps in this song.
Take care to sing them correctly.

More lah–me practice   p.58

Composing and writing

1 Prepare a new staff for writing on. Choose a position for Ⓢ, for example like this:

2 Make up a rhythm to fill the four bars. Speak your rhythm, and write it above the staff. For example:

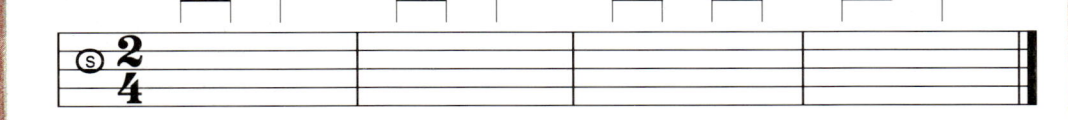

3 Now make up a melody based on your rhythm, using lah, soh and me. Sing it to a steady tempo.

lah   soh
  me

4 Write your singing names as noteheads (𝅝) on the staff.

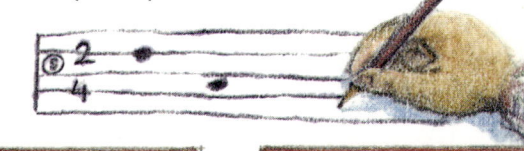

5 Add the rhythm (stems) to your notes. Now you can see your melody in staff notation. Ask a partner to read and sing your melody.

16 Composing melodies in staff notation   p.58   8

Rhythm echoes

This rhythm is for two performers.

Tap a steady pulse and speak the rhythm names of the upper part.

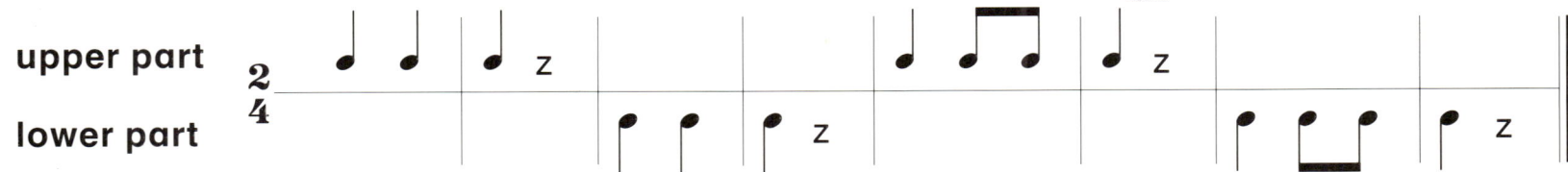

You need a partner to perform this piece with you.

Agree a tempo, and perform the piece by speaking rhythm names.

Now do the same for the lower part.

Can you see that the lower part is copying the upper part?

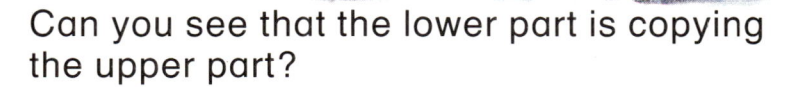

Now, perform the piece on two different percussion instruments.

Two-part rhythms (1)   p.59

Rhythm conversations

In this rhythm piece, the upper part is quite different from the lower part.

With a partner, practise each part separately.

This is my part.

My part is quite different.

Then decide which part each will perform.

Now perform the piece on two different instruments. Try making some similar rhythm pieces of your own:

Piece 1 – with the lower part copying the upper part

Piece 2 – with the upper part copying the lower part

Piece 3 – with the lower part different from the upper part

Work in 2-bar phrases.

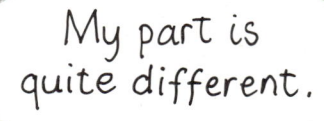

18 Two-part rhythms (2)   p.59   9

Two-part rhythms

Here are more two-part rhythm pieces.

The lower part does not always wait
for the upper part to finish,
so sometimes both parts sound together.

...and we both finish together!

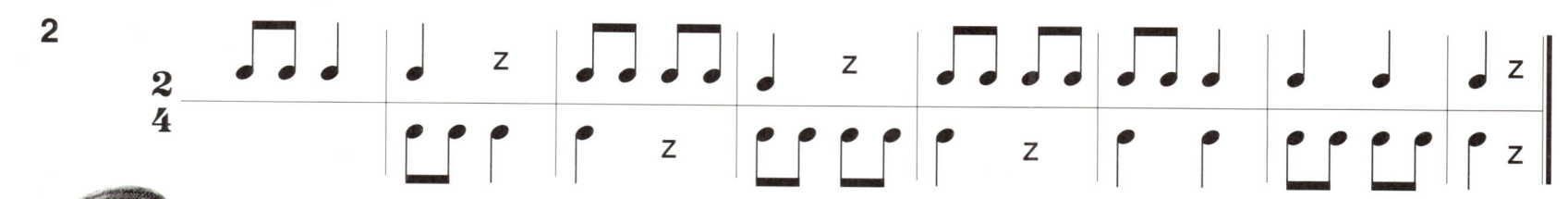

This sounds good!

Perform these rhythm pieces with your partner, either speaking the rhythms or using two different percussion instruments.

Take turns to perform the upper and lower parts.

Notice the number of phrases in each part.

Two-part rhythms (3)   p.60

Which melody?

Choose one of these melodies and hum it to a partner.

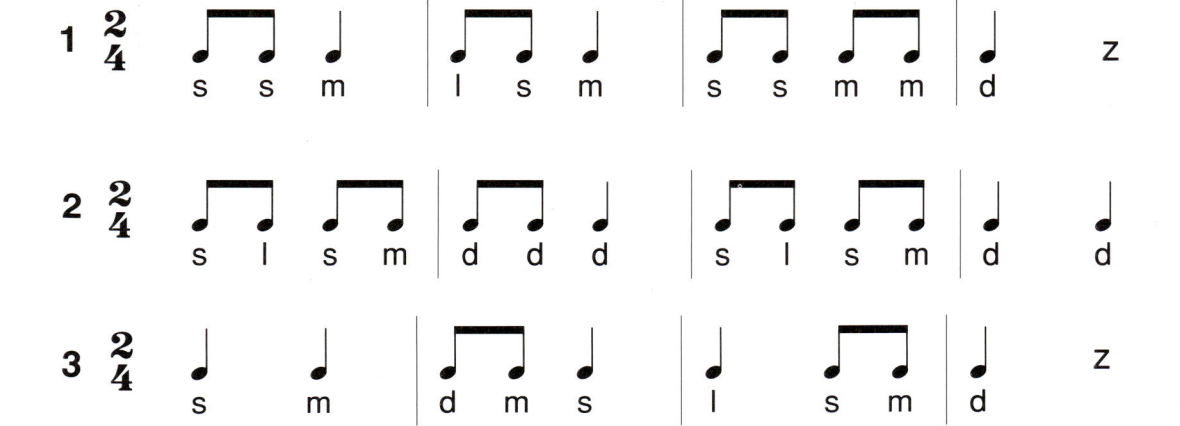

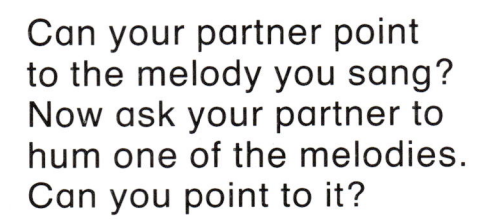

1. 2/4 | s s m | l s m | s s m m | d z |

2. 2/4 | s l s m | d d d | s l s m | d d |

3. 2/4 | s m | d m s | l | s m d z |

Can your partner point to the melody you sang? Now ask your partner to hum one of the melodies. Can you point to it?

If you close the book, can you sing your melodies to each other from memory?

With a partner, sing both of these melodies.
Which melody has a phrase which is repeated?

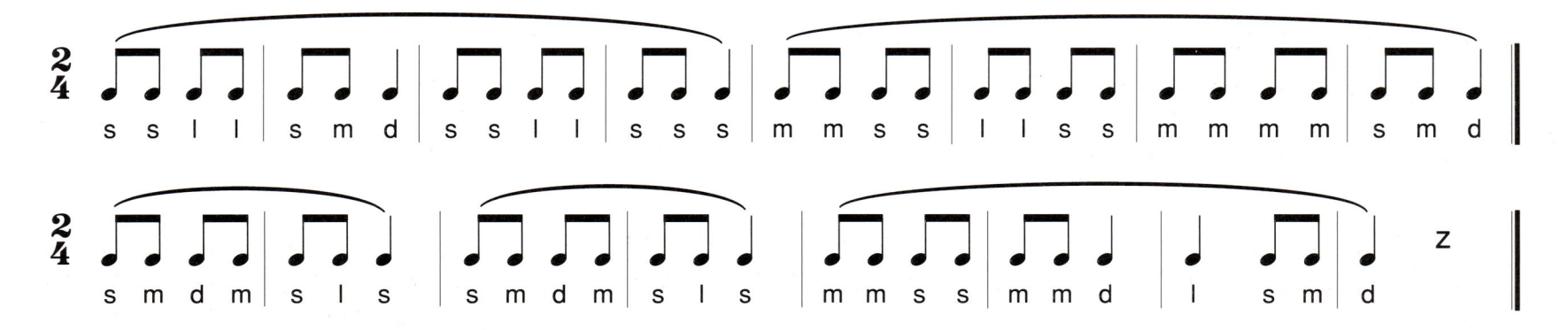

2/4 | s s l l | s m d | s s l l | s s s | m m s s | l l s s | m m m m | s m d ||

2/4 | s m d m | s l s | s m d m | s l s | m m s s | m m d | l | s m d z |

20 Reading l–s–m–d melodies   p.60

me

ray

doh

Sing this melody:

d d d | r r r | m m m m | r r d

It uses three notes: me, ray, doh.
It has one phrase.

This me–ray–doh melody has three phrases:

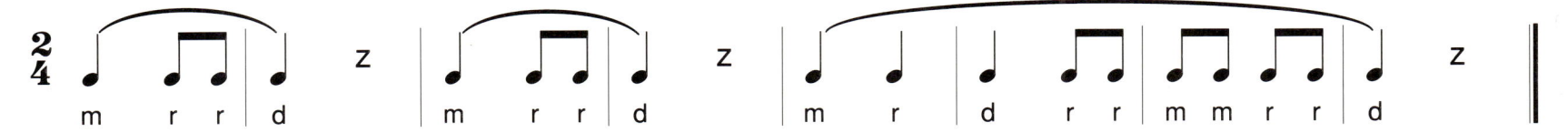

m r r d | m r r d | m r d | r r m m r r d

Point to the phrases which are the same.

Using m–r–d, make two new melodies using this 8-bar rhythm:

For Melody 1, make the second phrase the same as the first.
For Melody 2, make the second phrase different from the first.

From memory play your two melodies on a melodic instrument (with doh = c).

Constructing m–r–d melodies   p.60

Song Bus

Here are two Song Buses. Sing their melodies.
Then, choose a new starting note and sing them again.

> Later, sing the second song like this:
>
> Bars 1 and 2 – 'thinking' voice
> Bars 3 and 4 – 'singing' voice
> Bars 5 and 6 – 'thinking' voice
> Bars 7 and 8 – 'singing' voice
> Bars 9 and 10 – 'thinking' voice
> Bars 11 and 12 – 'singing' voice
>
> What do you notice when you do this?

THE 8 - BAR BUS Co.

m m r d   d r r m   s m m r   d d r m d

THE 12 - BAR BUS Co.

ssmm rrmm ssmm rrdd ssmm rrmm ssmm rrdd rrmm rrmm ssmm rrdd

Reading s–m–r–d melodies p.60

Two-phrase melodies

1 Ask a partner to make a 4-bar rhythm (2 beats to each bar).

2 Speak the rhythm together and write it down.

ti-ti ta ti-ti ti-ti ...

3 Then write down the rhythm again to make a second phrase.

You now have an 8-bar rhythm-piece.

4 Using soh, me, ray and doh, compose two melodies so that:

Melody 1 has two phrases which are the same.
Melody 2 has two phrases which are different.
(They will have the same rhythm but a different melody.)

Soh soh me me doh ray doh

Does your partner like what you have done?

5 From memory, play your melodies on a keyboard instrument (doh = C).

Composing s–m–r–d melodies   p.60   7

Song Train

Here is a Song Train.
Sing the melody.

l s m r d

1	2	3	4
2/4 s m m r m s s	s m m r m d d	d m s s l l s	s m m r m d d

Each carriage is a phrase of the melody.

Look at the numbers on the carriages.
Suppose the carriages were arranged in a different order, for instance 1, 4, 2, 3, then how would the melody sound?

Change the order of the carriages again.

How many different melodies can you make?

l–s–m–r–d (the doh pentatone)   p.61

On the ladder

Starlight Starbright

s l s m | s l l s s m | m r m | m s m | m r m s | m r d

Read and sing the 'Starlight' melody.
Notice how it moves only one step at a time,
up and down the l–s–m–r–d ladder.

Tom Cats

Read and sing the 'Tom cats' melody.
Notice how often it jumps a step on the ladder.

s m | d d m | s s m l | s s m | s m | d d m s | m r | d z

More doh pentatone melodies p.61

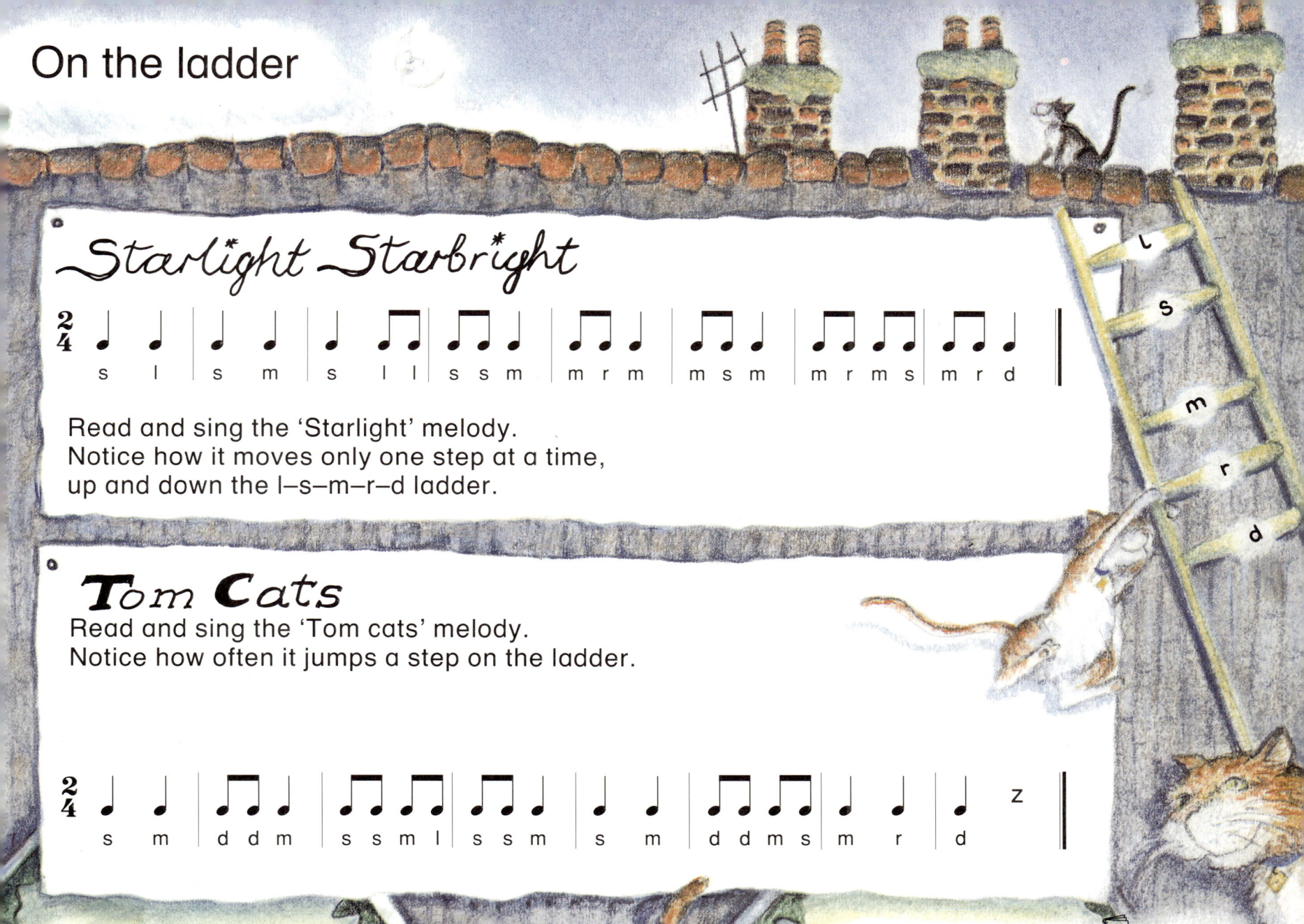

Musical conversations

Read and sing with a partner.

When your part has no melody, follow the other part with your 'thinking' voice.

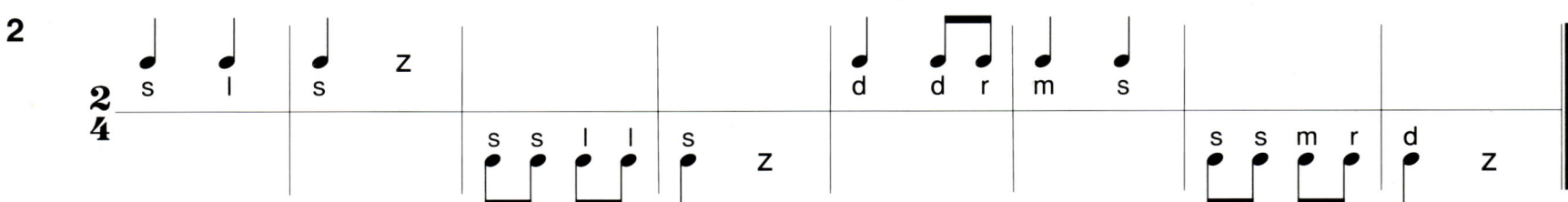

This Song Bus is a double-decker. There is an upper part and a lower part.

If you change tempo for each performance, you can make the Song Bus go faster or slower.

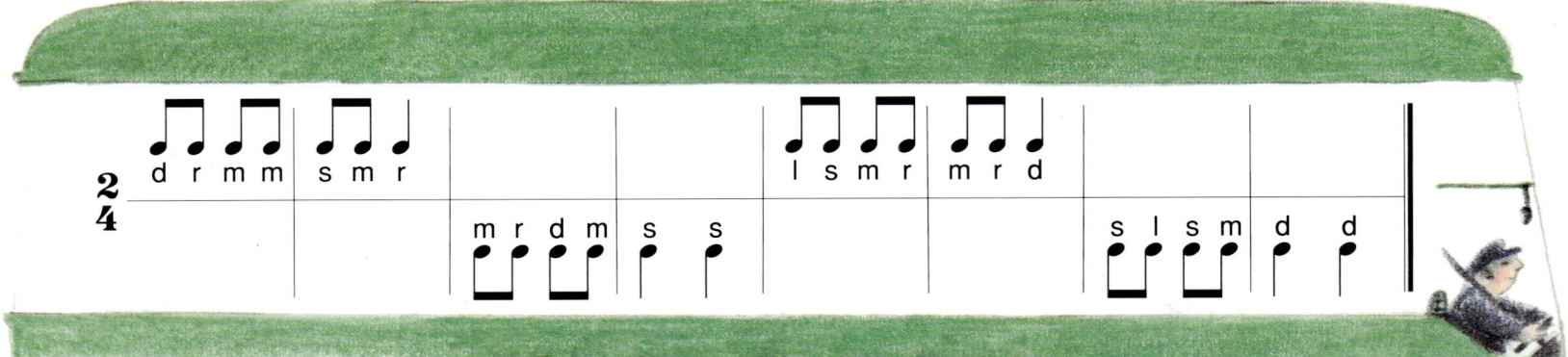

Reading in two parts (1) p.62

Two-part singing

Melody Factory

With your partner, read and sing these two-part pieces.

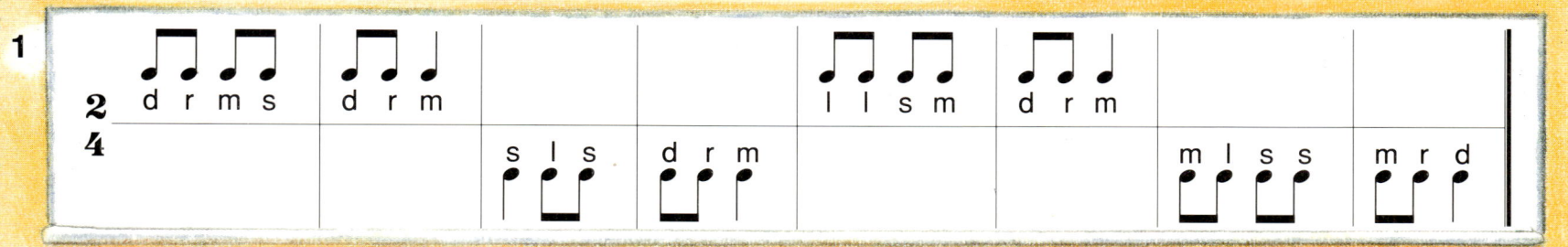

1. 2/4 | d r m s | d r m | | l l s m | d r m |
        | | s l s | d r m | | m l s s | m r d |

The next piece isn't just a musical conversation.
In the last three bars the two parts must sound at the same time.

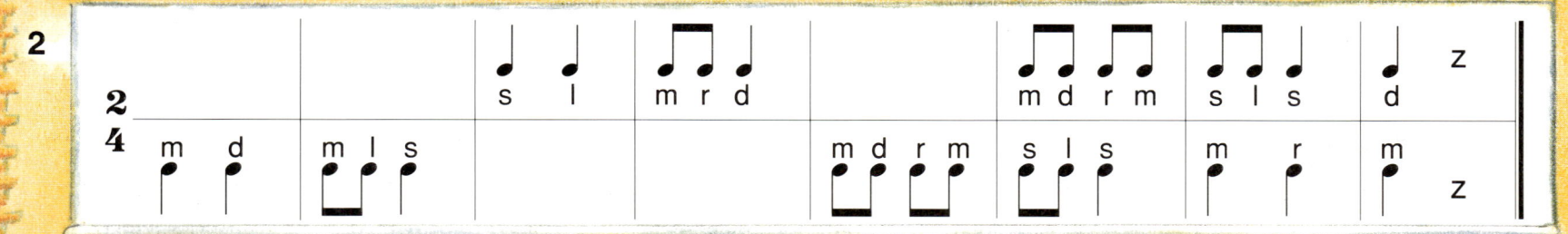

2. 2/4 | | s l | m r d | | m d r m | s l s | d z |
        | m d | m l s | | | m d r m | s l s | m r m z |

Watch out for the rests! Take a breath at each rest.

3. 2/4 | s s l | s z | s s m r | d z | m d r | m l s | s s m r | d z |
        | | s s l | s z | d d r | m z | m d r | m s | m r d |

Reading in two parts (2)   p.62   27

Add the lower part

You are now ready to compose your own two-part melody by adding a lower part.

First of all, copy this down:

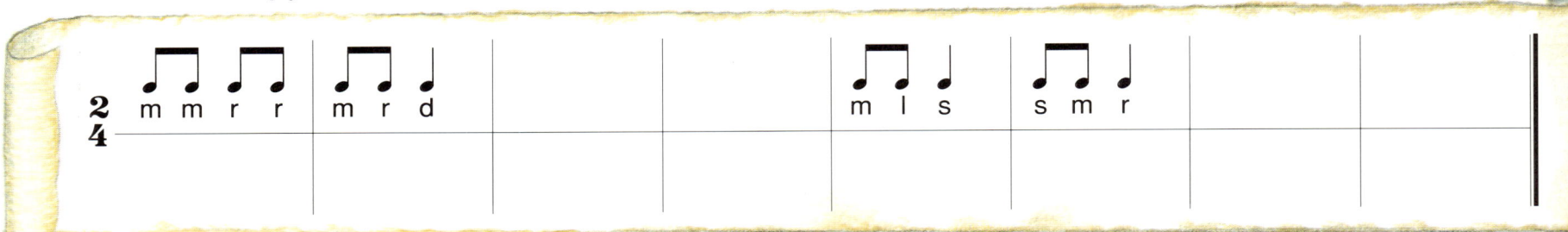

$\frac{2}{4}$ m m r r | m r d | | | m l s | s m r | |

Read and sing the upper part. Make sure you leave the correct gap between the two phrases.

Now make a lower part which fits between the phrases of the upper part.

1 Make the lower part in bars 3 and 4 the <u>same</u> as the upper part in bars 1 and 2.

BARS 1-2
BARS 3-4

2 But make the lower part in bars 7 and 8 <u>different</u> from the upper part in bars 5 and 6.

BARS 5-6
BARS 7-8

Composing in two parts (1)   p.62   9

Composing in two parts

Copy this on to your Writing Sheet:

This time you only have an upper part rhythm to start with.

Now make your own two-part piece, using 2-bar phrases as before (l–s–m–r–d).
Decide whether the lower part phrases will be the same as the upper part, or different.

1 Sing the phrases with your 'thinking' voice <u>before</u> writing them down.

Lah lah soh soh doh soh me ...

2 Ask a partner to perform the piece with you.

Composing in two parts (2)　p.62　9

me – ray – doh on the staff

Look at the position of ⓓ, which shows where **doh** is on the staff.

Tap the rhythm... then sing the melody.

*Sing the melody quietly.
Sing the melody loudly.
Sing the melody slowly.
Sing the melody quickly.*

Read and sing this melody with a partner.
Notice the position of the doh clef ⓓ on the staff.

With your partner, can you sing this melody as a canon?
The second part starts from the beginning when the first singer reaches ✳ (bar 2).

m–r–d on the staff; the doh clef   p.65

Suo-gân

Here is a beautiful Welsh lullaby:

You will need a slow tempo to sing the baby to sleep.

Each bar has the same ♫ ♩ rhythm.

Phrases 1 and 2 are the same as phrases 3 and 4.

Su - o - gân, do not weep, Su - o - gân, go to sleep.

Su - o - gân, have no fear, Su - o - gân, mo-ther's near.

1 Compose a me-ray-doh lullaby with the same phrase pattern as the Welsh melody. This time each bar should have this rhythm: ♩ ♫

2 Write your lullaby in staff notation.

3 Write words for your lullaby.

Staff notation m–r–d   p.65   8

Jigsaw puzzle

Sing all the phrases on the jigsaw pieces.

These five short phrases use lah-soh-me.

These five short phrases use me-ray-doh.

- Choose four phrases and decide in which order you will sing them.

  Sing your four phrases to a partner.

  Can your partner improve your melody by exchanging one picture only?

- Construct a melody using eight jigsaw phrases (phrases may be used more than once).

  First, use l–s–m and m–r–d phrases alternately.
  Then use l–s–m and m–r–d phrases in an order of your own choice.

  Invent other structures using these jigsaw phrases.

Building melodies from 2-bar phrases   p.65   8